DATE DUE

JY 8 '93			
JY 29 '93			
APR 21 '9?			
MAY 02 '9?			
JY 19 '02			
JY 15 '03			
JY 30 '03			
AG 03 '0?			
JY 14 '0?			
FE 02 '??			
SE 08 '??			
MR 03 '??			

12,401

Hallinan, P. K.
  How really great to walk this way, by P. K.
Hallinan; illus. by Jim Buckley. Childrens
Press, c1972.
  31p. col.illus.

1.Play. I.Illus. II.Title.

HoW ReaLLY GReaT

TO WALK THIS WAY

By P. K. Hallinan

Illustrations by Jim Buckley

CHILDRENS PRESS, CHICAGO

Library of Congress Catalog Card Number: 73-178496

6 7 8 9 10 11 12 13 14 15 16 17 18 19 20 21 22 23 24 25 R 75 74

How really great
to walk this way . . .

or walk this way

or walk this way

4

or lie on the grass

on a warm summer day . . . .

or do nothing at all
if you feel that way.

How really great
to stand on your head

or sit on your hands . . .

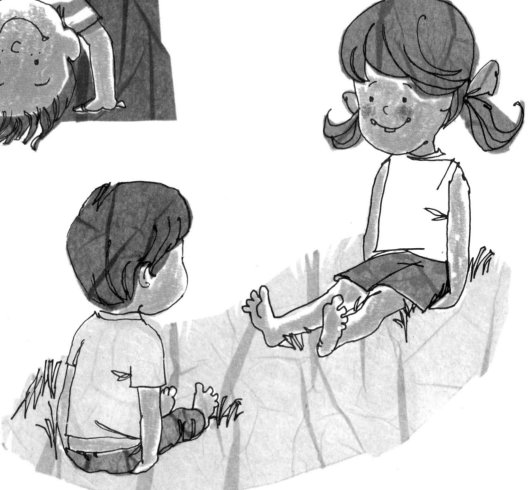

or lie on your bed

or think big thoughts

for hours and hours . . .

or smell a small handful
of beautiful flowers.

How really great

to play in the dirt . . .

or run in the sand

or wear an old shirt . . .

or run unafraid

from a giant blue wave

14

or sit in a cave
like an Indian brave.

How really great
just laughing out loud

or catching some raindrops

or watching a cloud . . .

or whistling a whistle

while the sun's going down

or sitting on the ground
with leaves all around.

How really great
just finding a stone

or being with someone . . .

or being alone

or listening to a shell
that you found by the sea

or planting a seed
that will grow a new tree.

How really great
to drink from a stream

or be in the woods . . .

or see a moonbeam

or blow on a dandelion
when the wind is soft
and watch the small spores
sail lightly aloft.

How really great
to feel your hair

or breathe the air

or see a bear.

How really great

to walk and say . . .

"How really great
to walk this way!"